Picture Credits
t=top, tr=top right, tl=top left, bl= bottom left, br=bottom right, b=bottom

Front Cover Images: Eric Isselée/ Shutterstock; Lisa F. Young/ Shutterstock; Istockphoto; Kitch Bain/ Shutterstock; Khramtsova Tatyana/ Shutterstock; Shutterstock; Eric Isselée/ Shutterstock; Q2AMedia Image Bank.

Back Cover Images: Edgewater Media/ Shutterstock (t); Eric Isselée/ Shutterstock (b).

P2-3: Klaas Lingbeek- van Kranen/ Istockphoto; P5: Edgewater Media/ Shutterstock (tr); P5: Shutterstock (b); P6-7: Rubiphoto/ Shutterstock (t); P7: Michael Klenetsky/ Dreamstime (t); P7: Ian Scott/ Fotolia (b); P8: Christian Musat/ Shutterstock; P10: Keith Levit/ Shutterstock (t); P10: Robert Cumming/ Shutterstock (b); P11: Kristian Sekulic/ Shutterstock; P12: Kesman/ Dreamstime; P12-13: James Kingman/ Shutterstock (t); P13: Pal Teravagimov/ Shutterstock; P14: Kitch Bain/ Shutterstock (t); P14: Simone van den Berg/ Istockphoto (b); P15: Donald Gargano/ Shutterstock (t); P15: Shutterstock (b); P16: Peter Betts/ Dreamstime; P16-17: Galina Barskaya/ Shutterstock (b); P17: Shutterstock; P18-19: Stephen Meese/ Shutterstock (t); P18: Yayatan/ Dreamstime (b); P19: Alain Couillaud/ Istockphoto (b); P20: Marsha Goldenberg/ Shutterstock (t); P20-21: Dennis Donohue/ Shutterstock (b); P21: Shutterstock; P22: 123RF; P22-23: Hans-Peter Naundorf/ Shutterstock (t); P23: Gordana Sermek/ Shutterstock; P24: Shutterstock; P25: Shutterstock (t); P25: Shutterstock (b); P26-27: luis Azevedo/ Istockphoto (t); P26: Alan Lucas/ Istockphoto (b); P27: Jason Stitt/ Shutterstock (tr); P27: Susan Flashman/ Shutterstock (b); P28: Dreamstime; P28-29: Nick Bell/ 123RF (t); P29: Eric Isselée/ Shutterstock (b); P30: Shutterstock (t); P30: Joel Kempson/ Dreamstime (b); P31: HYPERLINK "http://www.bigstockphoto.com/search/photographer/Mr.%20Lopez/" Mr. Lopez/ Bigstockphoto; P32: Shutterstock (t); P32: Fotolia (b); P33: HYPERLINK "http://www.bigstockphoto.com/search/photographer/ Frank%20Brouwer/" Frank Brouwer/ Bigstockphoto (t); P34: Bart Coenders/ Istockphoto (t); P34-35: Klaas Lingbeek- van Kranen/ Istockphoto; P35: Lilithlita/ Dreamstime (t); P36: HYPERLINK "http://www.shutterstock. com/gallery-4670p1.html" Edgewater Media/ Shutterstock (t); P36: Elzbieta Sekowska/ Shutterstock (b); P37: Rich Carey/ Shutterstock; P38-39: Kristian Sekulic/ Shutterstock (t); P38-39: Victoria Johnson (m); P38-39: Csaba Fikker/ 123RF (b); P39: Fotolia (b); P40: Luis Louro/ Fotolia (bl); P40: Kurt G/ Shutterstock (br); P41: Audrey Snider-Bell/ Shutterstock; P42-43: Dainis Derics/ Shutterstock (t); P42-43: Cathy Keifer/ Shutterstock (b); P43: Cathy Keifer/ Shutterstock; P 46-47: Klaas Lingbeek- van Kranen/ Istockphoto.
Q2AMedia Image Bank: 6; 9; 33; 44; 45.

Copyright: North Parade Publishing Ltd.
4 North Parade, Bath, BA1 1LF, UK

First Published: 2009
Designed and packaged by
Q2AMEDIA
Printed in China.

CONTENTS

ABOUT ANIMALS

Animals are a large group of multi-cellular organisms. They are different from human beings. Animals can be divided into five groups: mammals, reptiles, amphibians, birds and fish.

Some amphibians begin their life in the water. Frogs for example begin their life as tadpoles in the water.

Mammalia

There are more than 4,000 kinds of mammals in the world. They are warm-blooded animals and are found in all parts of the world. They are the most intelligent creatures on earth and can **adapt** their body temperature to different climatic conditions and temperatures.

Kangaroos belong to a class of mammals known as marsupials.

- The Black Swallower fish can swallow fish much larger in size than itself.

- Marsupials are mammals that have pouches and carry their young after they are born. Kangaroos, koalas and opossums are some common marsupials.

- Salamanders are amphibians, but are often mistaken for reptiles because they look similar to lizards. Salamanders have smooth skin and lack claws.

DID YOU KNOW?

To protect themselves, toads puff up their bodies to look larger than their original size.

Amphibians and Reptiles

Both amphibians and reptiles are cold-blooded animals that breathe through lungs. Amphibians, however, can also live underwater. Frogs and toads are amphibians while snakes and lizards are called reptiles.

Some frogs can even climb trees.

Frogs have two bulging eyes

All frogs have short front legs, long back legs and a stubby body

In Air and in Water

Birds are warm-blooded animals that lay eggs. Unlike other animals, birds can fly using wings. However, there are some birds, like the ostrich, that do not fly. Fish, on the other hand, stay only in water. They will die if they are taken out of water. They breathe through **gills**.

Some fish live in big groups called schools.

Fun Facts

Most mammals give birth to live young offspring. However, there are a few mammals, like the duck-billed platypus, that lay eggs instead of giving birth to their young.

7

CANINES

Canine (or Canidae) is the name for the dog family that includes wolves, foxes, coyotes and jackals. There are about 400 species of dog in the world.

The Fox

The fox is the most common mammal found in the world. It is much smaller than other canines. The fox is also a solitary animal, unlike many other canines that live in groups. The red fox is the most common species.

The sandy coloured coat of the Fennec fox allows it to blend into the desert surroundings.

A fox's large ears help to dissipate heat and detect movement.

Fun Facts

The Arctic fox is the only member of the Canidae family that changes the colour of its coat according to the season. While its winter coat is white, it has a bluish grey coat in summer.

The Fennec fox is the smallest fox in the world.

- The dingo is an Australian wild dog, found in all states of Australia except Tasmania.

- Wolves have two layers of fur. The first layer helps to repel water and dust while the second layer helps to keep the body warm.

- Fox hunting began as a sport in the 16th century in the UK.

Wolves

Wolves belong to the same family as domesticated dogs. They are found in remote forests and hunt in packs. They feed on large and medium-sized animals like sheep, pigs and deer. There are two main species of wolves - the red and the grey.

Grey wolves are the largest Canines.

DID YOU KNOW ?

Foxes store their food under leaves, snow or soil to eat later.

BIG CATS

The big cats are the largest members of the cat family and include tigers, lions, leopards and jaguars. They are distinguished by their ability to roar.

The Striped Prowler

The tiger is the largest member of the big cat family. They grow up to 4 m (13 ft) in length and weigh over 300 kg (660 lbs). They are **nocturnal** animals and hunt for their prey at night. They have strong eyesight and a keen sense of smell. There are five different species of tiger in the world.

The Royal Bengal tiger is found in the rainforests and grasslands of Bangladesh, Bhutan, Burma, China, India and Nepal.

The Royal Bengal tiger has orange and white fur with black stripes.

Second in Charge

The lion is the second largest living cat. Unlike other big cats, lions live in big groups of about 15 animals, known as a pride. Male lions are recognised by the thick mane of brown hair that encircles their head and neck.

Lions are the most social of the big cats, living in groups.

- Though the leopard is the smallest member of the big cat family, it is still the best and strongest climber of all the large cats.

- The Siberian tiger (also known as the Amur) is a rare species of the tiger family. Only 7,000 Siberians are left in the world today.

- Cougars, also known as panthers or pumas, are the largest cats that can purr!

Fun Facts

Tigers have more than a hundred stripes on their body but no two tigers have the same number and pattern of stripes.

DID YOU KNOW?

Lions are the laziest of all the big cats. They sleep and rest for more than 20 hours a day!

HOOVED ANIMALS

Hooved animals are also known as ungulates. They can be odd-toed or even-toed, depending on the number of toes.

The camel's large nostrils store water vapour and help prevent water loss.

Fun Facts

All camels have a very unique stomach. Unlike humans or other animals, their stomachs are divided into three compartments, helping them in the digestion of their food.

Ship of the Desert

Most camels live in the desert, but some species are found in other arid areas like mountains. They can survive for a long time without water. Their **hump** is made of fatty tissues, which helps them control their body temperature and also act as an energy reserve to help them withstand long periods of heat and dehydration.

- The wild bactrian camel is one of the rarest mammals in the world.

- Camel meat is very healthy since it has no cholesterol and very little fat.

- Oryx antelopes, found in deserts, have a unique system of cooling their blood before it reaches their brain. This helps them regulate their body temperature to cope with living in hot, dry conditions.

Antelopes often have large horns that spiral up from their head.

Deer horns are different from the antelope's; they can shed their antlers, which then grow again.

Hooving Around

Antelopes are hooved mammals with hollow horns. They can be found in a variety of habitats. However, most of them live in grasslands. Antelope horns are made of a hard substance called keratin and grow throughout their lives.

DID YOU KNOW ?

Camels were used by the Bedouins in war against the Persians in the 7th century B.C.

MONKEYS AND APES

Monkeys and apes are mammals. They belong to the same category that human beings are a part of – **primates.**

Orangutans are apes that live in the rainforests of Borneo and Sumatra.

Their Habitat

Monkeys are found in many types of habitat – from forests and deserts to grasslands and mountains. They are found in all parts of the world. Apes, however, live only in the rainforests of Africa and Asia.

A group of monkeys is called a troop.

Fun Facts

Chimpanzees have a cheeky trick of poking a long stick into an ant hill. When the ants have crawled onto the stick, the chimpanzee takes the stick out and licks up all the ants!

Some monkeys have long tails that help them hold on to branches as they swing between trees.

Their Differences

Monkeys are different from apes in many ways. Most monkeys have tails but apes do not have tails. Apes can use their hands to swing from branch to branch. Monkeys cannot do that. Instead, they run on the tree branches.

- A monkey's eyes are rounder and closer together than human eyes.
- In some monkeys, the arms are as long as the legs.
- Monkeys do not catch a cold!
- Experts say that vervet monkeys have their own language.

A male gorilla is more than ten times stronger than an average adult man.

Male gorillas typically have a patch of silver hair on their back.

Gorillas walk on all four limbs, putting pressure on their knuckles. This is called knuckle-walking.

DID YOU KNOW?

Monkeys eat bananas just like us. They first peel off the skin and then eat the fruit.

ELEPHANTS

Elephants are the largest living land animals. They live in secluded areas, far from human beings.

When travelling, elephants move in a single file.

Trunking Around

Elephants weigh between 90-120 kg (200-265 lbs) when they are born. Elephants live in small groups. They eat roots, bark, grass, leaves and fruit. They have been known to uproot entire trees to reach the fruit!

- Female elephants are fertile to have **offspring** up to the age of around 55.

- Elephants have a very acute sense of hearing.

- The size of an elephant's family depends on the amount of food available in the area and how well they get along with each other.

Close Cousins

The Asian elephant is smaller than its African counterpart and has smaller ears. Despite their weight, elephants walk very quietly, distributing their weight by a thick cushion of tissue on the base of their foot.

African elephants can be easily recognised by their large ears, sloping foreheads and large tusks.

Elephants can weigh as much as a minibus!

The tusks help in gathering food and carrying heavy objects.

Fun Facts

Elephants are very sensitive animals. If a baby elephant complains, the entire herd of elephants gathers around the baby to look after it, caress it and console it.

DID YOU KNOW ?

Elephants use their trunks like a pipe, filling it with water and pouring it into their mouth.

RHINOS AND HIPPOS

Rhinoceroses and hippopotamuses are also classified as ungulates or hooved animals. The hippo lives on riverbanks. The rhino has horns.

The rhino's horn is made of keratin and was traditionally used in Asian medicines.

River Horse

The hippo (literally meaning 'river horse') spends its days in water and comes to the land at night to eat. A hippo can spend long periods underwater, but typically surfaces every 3 to 5 minutes to breathe. They are native to Africa.

Hippos graze for over 4 hours a day.

Fun Facts

Even when a hippo is sleeping underwater, it raises its head to breathe without even waking up!

Horned Nose

Rhinos are huge, with most species weighing nearly one tonne! They have a large horn above the nose and a tough exterior skin between 1.5-5 cm (0.5-2 in) thick. There are five types of rhinos: white, black, Indian, Sumatran and Javan.

- Hippos often scare away their **predator**s by opening their mouth and showing their canines, which can grow up to 50 cm (20 in) in length.
- The Javan rhino is one of the rarest and most **endangered** animal in the world.
- Hippos secrete a red substance from their skin, which acts like a natural sunscreen.

The white rhino is the second largest land mammal in the world. It has two horns on its snout.

DID YOU KNOW?

Indian and Javan rhinos have only one horn. All the rest have two.

BEARS

Bears are solitary animals, usually active in the early morning or at dusk. Bears are usually found in parts of the Americas, Europe and Asia.

The grizzly bear, like other brown bears, can be distinguished by the hump on its back, made up of muscle. This bundle of muscles gives the bear the force to dig its forelimbs into its prey.

Bears are good at climbing trees and are great swimmers.

The Big Brown Bear

The brown bear can be found all over Europe, Asia and North America. Despite its name, some species can be brown, black and even blonde. Brown bears are very powerful animals and can break the necks of even large prey when they hunt.

Fun Facts

Hibernating female bears don't even wake up when they give birth to their cubs during winter. The baby bear cubs crawl into a position where they can feed themselves from their mother soon after birth.

White as Snow

Polar bears live around the Arctic Ocean. They have a thick layer of fat under their skin, which helps them keep warm in cold climates and also helps them float while swimming. They also have two layers of fur.

- While the brown bear, the black bear and the panda rely on fruit, nuts and berries as their primary source of food, it is only the Polar bear that is mainly carnivorous in nature, feeding on seals.
- Pandas do not hibernate like other species of bears
- The grizzly bear is the largest meat eater in the world.

Despite their size, bears are fast runners.

The Polar bear lives mainly on seal meat.

The grizzly bear gets its name from the grey or silver tips of the hair on its back.

DID YOU KNOW?

Brown bears eat almost continuously during the summer and autumn as they get ready for winter.

RODENTS

Rodents are the largest order of mammals in terms of number of species. They have sharp incisor teeth that grow continuously and must be kept short by gnawing. They are found everywhere except in Antarctica.

Notorious Nibblers

Mice are the most common rodents and are found across the world. They typically prefer seeds and grains. They can also survive for long periods of time with little or no water, obtaining their water from the food that they eat. They are mainly nocturnal animals.

- Hamsters are named after the German word, *hamstern*, which means to hoard. This is due to the fact that these creatures carry food in their cheek pouches and hide it away safely.

- Pet gerbils have to be provided with things they can chew to prevent their very sharp incisors from growing too long.

Mice are usually most active at night.

Gentle Guinea Pigs

Small rodents like hamsters, gerbils and guinea pigs have become popular as family pets. Guinea pigs are the largest of all pet rodents. They are considered to be very good pets and seldom bite or scratch even if stressed or disturbed. They vary widely in hair composition and colour. Some have a smooth coat while others have a ruffled coat.

Fun Facts

Guinea pigs jump excitedly when threatened. This movement is known as 'pop corning' and is a type of war dance to scare away predators and escape to safety.

The capybara is the world's largest rodent. It can grow as big as a dog.

If guinea pigs don't get food to chew on, they chew on their own hair or even on plastic or cloth.

Their mild nature makes guinea pigs very popular as pets.

DID YOU KNOW?

Millions of people died in Europe in the 14th century because of a terrible disease carried by rats and transmitted by fleas. This was known as the Black Death.

BIRDS

Birds are warm-blooded vertebrates that lay eggs. There are more than 10,000 living species of birds in the world. All birds have feathers, beaks and wings, but not all can fly.

Most birds are active in the day. However, some birds like the owl are active at night.

Fly Away

Flying allows birds to travel, hunt for food and avoid predators. Birds have a very light skeleton, strong flying muscles and wings. The shape and size of the wing determines the distance and type of flight for birds. Feathers provide insulation and help maintain body temperature.

- Many birds **migrate** during the winter season. This helps them live in warmer regions and also look for food sources and breeding grounds in warmer climates.
- Water birds have waterproof feathers, which help them stay warm and dry.
- Water birds also have webbed feet which help them to paddle in the water.

Their Diet

While most birds are plant eating creatures, there are some birds that are meat eating. These are known as raptors or birds of prey. Vultures, hawks, eagles and kites are all birds of prey.

Female raptors are often larger than the males.

Raptors have sharp, curved beaks and strong feet with powerful claws.

Raptors have larger eyes than most other birds and have excellent colour vision.

Songbirds

Birds that have musical voices are called songbirds. They have specially developed vocal cords or syringes, which they use to produce sounds or 'songs'. They also have a special section in their brain which helps them learn their songs.

DID YOU KNOW ?

Some songbirds can even sing two songs at the same time.

FLIGHTLESS BIRDS

While most birds can fly, there are some birds that do not fly. Even though they look like birds, their legs are adapted in many instances to help them cover long distances by walking or running.

A kiwi may be the size of a chicken, but its egg is up to six times larger than a chicken's!

Running Bird

The ostrich is the largest flightless bird in the world. Found in parts of Africa, they weigh 113-181 kg (250-400 lbs) and stand 1.8-2.4 m (6-8 ft) tall. They have two-toed feet that allow them to run fast and escape from predators.

The long neck of the ostrich gives it the ability to see a greater distance across the plains.

- To produce her huge egg, the female kiwi must eat three times her normal food intake for a month!

- Emus, like the ostrich, drink large quantities of water and can drink up to 70 mouthfuls of water at one go.

- Contrary to popular belief, ostriches do not bury their head in the sand when they see danger.

Second in Size

The emu is the second-largest flightless bird and is commonly found in Australia. Weighing around 68 kg (150 lbs), a large emu can grow up to 1.5-1.8 m (5-6 ft) in height. Emus also have strong legs for running long distances.

Ostriches have small wings, with claws at the end that help them when they attack predators.

New Zealander

The kiwi is also a flightless bird. This protected and endangered national bird of New Zealand is nocturnal by nature. The kiwi's beak is almost one-third the length of its body. It uses its excellent sense of smell to hunt for worms, insects, berries and seeds.

DID YOU KNOW?

Emu eggs are dark green in colour. Each egg can weigh up to 0.68 kgs (1.5 lbs).

27

REPTILES

Reptiles are cold-blooded animals and are covered with scales or plates, as apposed to skin or feathers. The majority of reptiles are **oviparous**, meaning they lay eggs, from which their young are born.

- Four main orders of reptiles are recognised: **Crocodilia** (including crocodiles and alligators); **Sphenodontia** (including tuatara); **Squamata** (including lizards and snakes); **Testudines** (including turtles and tortoises).

- Most reptiles lay eggs, but some lizards and snakes give birth to live young.

- The horned lizard is known to defend itself from its enemies by spraying them with blood from the corner of its eye.

Komodo dragons can eat up to 80 per cent of their body weight during a single meal.

Slithering Around

Lizards make up the largest group of reptiles. There are over 3,700 species of lizards spread all over the world. Lizards also have dry, scaly skin and clawed feet. They usually feed on insects, with some being vegetarians.

The Komodo dragon is the largest lizard in the world.

The mouth of the Komodo dragon is full of poisonous bacteria capable of killing a man.

Mobile Homes

Turtles are also classified as reptiles. They have a hard shell on their back that acts like armour. Most turtles live in the sea. Turtles also have a beak but do not have any teeth. Their hard jaw rim helps them cut and chew food. Tortoises also belong to the same family as turtles but live on land.

Tortoises can draw their head, legs and tails into their hard shell when they sense danger.

Fun Facts

The average life span of a common snapping turtle is about 40 years. However, the giant tortoise is known to live for as long as 170 years!

DID YOU KNOW?

Chameleons have an amazing ability to change the colour of their body instantly.

SNAKES

Snakes are also reptiles, but they do not have legs. They are cold-blooded and usually nocturnal in nature. Some species, however, can be found in the day.

Slithering Around

Snakes do not have external ears but can sense sound through **vibrations**. They have an inner ear and can feel the vibrations on the ground. The vibration is then passed onto the inner ear and helps them hunt. They also have smell sensors on the tips of their tongues and heat sensors, which help them in locating food.

Some snakes have a flap of skin on the side of their head. These flare out to form a hood and help scare predators away.

Fun Facts

Snakes do not hear a snake charmer. When we see a snake swaying to the music of the snake charmer it is actually moving to the vibrations of the charmer's movement.

Snakes have a transparent scale that covers the eye. The scale is frequently replaced by a new one helping the snake see clearly again.

Snakes have a flexible lower jaw that helps them swallow their prey whole.

Snakes use their nostrils only for breathing. They smell with their tongues.

- The cottonmouth snake gets its name from the inner white lining of its mouth, which is exposed when it opens its mouth when sensing danger.

- Anacondas are semi-aquatic snakes believed to grow to great lengths.

- Rattlesnakes get their name from the loose scales at the end of their tail that makes a rattling noise under rapid vibration.

Boas are solitary and nocturnal snakes.

Crushing Machine

Many species of snakes are poisonous and kill their prey with their **venom**. However, some snakes, like the python, kill their prey by **constriction**; they coil their body around the prey and then slowly crush it. They then swallow the prey whole.

DID YOU KNOW?

Snakes have only one functional lung located on the right side of their body.

AMPHIBIANS

Amphibians can live on both land and in water. Most amphibians begin their life in water. Even fully grown, they cannot live all their life on land.

In Land and Water

Frogs, toads, and salamanders are all types of amphibians. Most amphibians are born in water, where the eggs are laid. Amphibians that are spawned in water do not have limbs and look more like fish. They breathe through gills and have tails to help them swim. Over time, their lungs and legs grow in a process known as **metamorphosis**.

A newt is a salamander that lives in the water as an adult.

Fun Facts

Most frogs live in and around water. However, there are also some types of frogs that never go near water and live only on land and even on trees, extracting moisture from the air!

There are more than 6,000 species of amphibians in the world.

Frog Story

Frogs are found in most parts of the world. Almost all species of frogs have long back legs and shorter front legs, which help them to move. Frogs are usually green in colour, but many also have colourful markings on their body.

Most frogs have large bulging eyes.

The skin of frogs has the ability to absorb water.

- Salamanders are short-legged amphibians, usually with long tails.
- Newts are a type of salamander and may be fully- or semi-aquatic.
- Frogs catch live prey by darting out their long, sticky tongue. The marine toad eats plants as well as scavenged flesh.

Their strong back legs help frogs leap to safety whenever they sense danger.

DID YOU KNOW ?

Some rainforest frogs are very poisonous. This poison has traditionally been used to tip arrows and darts.

SHARKS AND RAYS

The great white shark is the most feared of all sharks.

Sharks and rays are among some of the most feared and misunderstood creatures in the seas and oceans.

Sharks use their tail to provide thrust and speed while swimming.

Fun Facts

Hammerhead sharks are named because of the unusual shape of their heads. Shaped like a hammer, the wide head places the eyes far apart and helps with hunting.

Predators at Sea

Sharks are a type of fish. They do not have bones like other fish but are made up of cartilage – strong tissue as hard as bone. Sharks have a keen sense of smell and some can detect just a drop of blood from quite a distance. Many sharks also have keen eyesight.

Poisonous Sting

Stingrays are related to sharks and get their name from the **serrated**, poisonous spine that grows from their tail. Stingrays can grow as long as 4.6 m (15 ft). However, they normally only sting only in **self defence**.

Stingrays spend most of their time inactive, buried in the sand on the ocean floor.

- Stingrays are a family of fish and include several different species.
- There are about 368 species of sharks in the world.
- Some shark species are **oviparous** (egg-layers) and some are **viviparous**, giving birth to live pups.

The whale shark is the largest shark. It is also the largest fish in the world and can grow up to 15 m (50 ft) long!

CRABS AND SHELLFISH

Crustacea and molluscs are another type of marine life. They include crabs, lobsters, shrimps, and crayfish. The octopus is a type of mollusc.

Crustacea

The crab and the lobster are some of the most popular crustacea in the world. They have a soft inner body and a hard outer shell called an **exoskeleton**. The shell does not grow in size; rather, the outer shell is shed at regular intervals as a larger shell develops beneath.

The horseshoe crab has changed very little in over 25 million years.

A crab's claws are known as chelae.

Fun Facts

The octopus uses a substance called haemocyanin to transport oxygen around its body. This makes its blood look blue and not red!

Prey Suckers

The octopus is an invertebrate with a bag-shaped body, a large head and eight tentacles used to catch prey. Octopuses have the remarkable ability to change both the colour and the texture of their body. This helps them to merge into their surroundings and escape from enemies. Snails and slugs also belong to the same family as the octopus.

- Each tentacle of the octopus has one or two rows of suction pads that help them capture prey.
- Young squid spawn in great numbers and are sometimes nicknamed the 'ice-cream cones of the sea'.
- Horseshoe crabs are not really crabs but are more closely related to spiders.

The octopus squirts out a black inky substance when it is threatened. It uses the resulting cloud to make its escape.

DID YOU KNOW?

Crabs walk sideways because their leg muscles can only retract and pull.

MARINE MAMMALS

There are about 120 species of mammals in the world that can be classified as marine mammals, including whales, dolphins and walruses.

A whale's tail fin is horizontal and not vertical like a shark's.

Whales

Whales are among the biggest living creatures in the world. Whales are warm-blooded and give birth to live young. They breathe air through lungs and have to surface at regular intervals to breathe in through blowholes situated on top of their heads. Baleen whales have a sieve-like structure, which they use to separate plankton from the water. The toothed whales have teeth and eat fish and squid.

- Dolphins and whales use sound waves to locate their food and other objects in the water.
- The killer whale (orca) is actually the largest dolphin and can grow up to 6.1 m (20 ft) long.
- The average bottlenose dolphin brain weighs 1.5 kgs (3.4 lbs) more than the human brain.

Dolphins

Dolphins belong to the same family (**cetaceans**) as whales but are physically different from them. They can be found in all oceans and seas and feed on small fish, squid, crabs, shrimps and lobsters. Dolphins are also social animals and live in large groups of 12 or more animals. These groups are known as pods.

Seals and Walruses

Walruses and seals are flippered mammals and belong to the family of pinnipeds. Walruses live in the Arctic Ocean and sub-Arctic seas of the Northern Hemisphere. Seals live in the Antarctic region.

Although they live in saltwater, dolphins do not drink water. They get their water from their food.

Dolphins are playful creatures, often racing through the water and jumping out of it.

Fun Facts

Dolphins have to be conscious to breath, meaning they can never fall asleep completely. Instead, they let one half of their brain sleep at a time.

DID YOU KNOW?

Dolphins can produce unique whistles that help individual dolphins recognise each other.

SPIDERS AND SCORPIONS

Spiders and scorpions belong to the family of arachnids. There are over 100,000 species of arachnids in the world. They are different from insects in many ways, including having eight legs instead of six.

Web Masters

Spiders are found in all parts of the world and in every kind of habitat. They can be found in many colours. They are carnivores and hunt their prey through their sticky webs or by other clever traps.

Most spiders are extremely sensitive to sound and vibrations.

Spiders do not have claws but some have poisonous fangs.

The body of a spider is divided into two main parts, the thorax and abdomen.

Not all spiders are a dull black or brown.

Fun Facts

Some spiders have stripes and blotches on their body. This is a technique called *disruptive colouration* and helps them merge into the background and escape from predators.

- Scorpions usually eat insects. When food is scarce they have the amazing ability to slow down their metabolism and eat one third their normal amount of food.

- Though scorpions can live without food and even in harsh conditions, they cannot survive in areas where there is no loose soil.

- The jumping spider gets more than 90 per cent of its food from solid plant material produced by acacias.

Pincer Attack

Scorpions are closely related to spiders, mites and ticks. Scorpions are found in deserts, in the Brazilian rainforests and even the Himalayan mountains! Most scorpions are nocturnal by nature and (contrary to popular belief) are not aggressive towards humans, unless provoked!

Scorpions navigate using sensory hairs and slit organs on their legs.

DID YOU KNOW?

There are almost 2,000 species of scorpions but only 30-40 species are poisonous enough to kill a human.

CREEPY CRAWLIES

Insects make up the largest group of creatures on earth. Eight out of every ten of all species are insects!

A queen bee can lay over 1,000 eggs in a day.

Hard Life

Insects are **arthropods**, meaning they have joint legs and a tough cover known as an exoskeleton outside their body. Confusingly, all insects are arthropods but not all arthropods are insects! The hard exoskeleton supports the body of the insect and helps protect the soft inner parts.

Fun Facts

When the bee larva is fed a diet of royal jelly, it grows into a queen bee. The other larvae are only fed royal jelly for two days. Then they are given pollen and honey.

- Insects that live in large colonies are known as social insects. Ants and bees are social insects.
- Different insects lay their eggs in different places. While some lay their eggs inside plant stems, some insects, like the beetle, lay their eggs on dead animals.
- Some insects, including mosquitos, lice and bedbugs are known as pests. However, there are some that are helpful to us, such as bees.

While some insects have simple eyes, most have compound eyes consisting of six-sided lenses.

Insects use their head to eat, feel their way around and even gather information through a pair of antennae.

Many insects, such as butterflies, have two pairs of wings on the sides of their bodies.

Parts and More

Most insects are born as eggs and grow into a larva, called a nymph. The larva becomes a pupa before becoming an adult. An insect's body consists of the head, thorax and abdomen. The head has a pair of antennae, eyes and a mouth. The thorax supports the legs and wings while the abdomen helps digest food.

DID YOU KNOW?

Insects breathe through their trachea and small holes on their sides.

GLOSSARY

Adapt: to change according to the situation and circumstance

Endangered: something that is in danger of vanishing from the Earth

Gills: respiratory organ of animals that live in water

Hump: something that bulges out

Migrate: move from one region to another

Nocturnal: animals that are active during the night

Offspring: babies; the young of an animal

Predator: animal that hunts

Primate: an animal group that includes monkeys

Self defence: to protect oneself

Serrated: having a row of sharp, saw-like teeth

Venom: poisonous substance secreted by some animals

Vibration: move back and forth in a rapid manner

INDEX